STILL MORE OF
WHO SAID THAT?

Quotations and biographies
of famous people

Selected and compiled by
RENIE GEE

David & Charles
Newton Abbot London North Pomfret (Vt)

British Library Cataloguing in Publication Data

Still more of who said that?
  1. Quotations, English   2. Biography
  I. Gee, Renie
  080   PN6081

  ISBN 0–7153–8475–9

Typeset by Photo-Graphics, Honiton, Devon
and printed in Great Britain by
A. Wheaton & Co, Hennock Road, Exeter
for David & Charles (Publishers) Limited
Brunel House Newton Abbot Devon

Published in the United States of America
by David & Charles Inc
North Pomfret   Vermont 05053   USA

Introduction

I have found to my delight that research can be enjoyable, rewarding and a stimulus for yet more research. Never an enthusiast for history at school, I now find that unearthing personalities from behind the facades of dates and history books can be a fascinating job. For example, from the meetings of the London Literary Club in Fleet Street there are records of the opinions aired amongst the contemporary literary circles. Noted down for posterity, these records provide us with a valuable insight into the sayings and doings of the mid-eighteenth century. In much the same way the Romans did this when they established records of rules and regulations for occupied Britain. The Sages' reports from the period before Christ similarly reflected their own era.

These people and their friends come gloriously alive to me as I read their accounts and I often quote from them.

This latest collection of quotations includes examples of presentday writers. You will find sayings such as the Duke of Edinburgh's comment: 'It is no good shutting your eyes and saying "British is Best" three times a day after meals, and expecting it to be so', J.B. Priestley's 'Standard English is tasteless stuff', as well as Dorothy Dix's pert 'Drying a widow's tears is one of the most dangerous occupations known to man'.

I have been asked by friends to include Martin Luther King and G.K. Chesterton in this latest book, and this I gladly do. I hope your pleasure in reading it will equal my own in compiling it.

RENIE GEE

To Gordon
With love and best wishes for his future

Joseph Addison

There was a Club of Fat Men that did not come together to entertain one another with Sprightliness and Wit, but to keep one another in Countenance.

The room where the Club met was something of the largest and had two Entrances, one by a Door of moderate Size and the other by a pair of Folding Doors. If a Candidate for this Corpulent Club could make his Entrance through the first he was looked upon as unqualified...

... if he stuck in the Passage and could not force his way through it, the Folding Doors were thrown open for his Reception, and he was saluted as a Brother.

In opposition to this Society there sprung up another, composed of Scare-Crows and Skeletons...

...At length they come to this Accommodation, that the two Bailiffs of the Town should be annually chosen out of the two Clubs; by which the principal Magistrates are at this Day coupled like Rabbits, one fat and one lean.

On Clubs, The Spectator

Joseph Addison (1672–1719) was a British essayist and poet. Born in Wiltshire, he was granted a pension to enable him to qualify for the Diplomatic Service by foreign travel, and in 1704 he celebrated Marlborough's victory at Blenheim in his poem *The Campaign*. He became Under-Secretary of State, Secretary to the Lord Lieutenant of Ireland and an MP, and helped to establish *The Spectator*.

Hans Christian Andersen

Where words fail, music speaks.

Quoted in Reader's Digest, March 1980

Hans Christian Andersen (1805–85) was a Danish writer. The son of a shoemaker, he was born at Odense and his first book was published when he was only seventeen but it was not until 1829 that he attracted notice. In 1835 his novel *The Improvisatore* brought him popularity and he began to compose the immortal fairy tales which have since been translated into a great many languages.

Margot Asquith

He has a brilliant mind until he makes it up.
of Sir Stafford Cripps

She tells enough white lies to ice a cake.
of a female acquaintance

I saw him riding in the Row, clinging to his horse like a string of onions.
of Lord Hugh Cecil

Very clever, but his brains go to his head.
of F.E. Smith

She's as tough as an ox. She'll be turned into OXO when she dies.
of a friend

Margot Asquith (1868–1945) was originally Margot Tennant, daughter of Sir Charles Tennant, a rich Glasgow industrialist. In 1894 she married into the famous Asquith family and became known as a celebrated wit, but her volumes of memoires offended many by their lack of reticence. As wife of the Liberal Prime Minister she had a wide circle of friends and acquaintances.

Hylda Baker

Punctuality is something that if you have it, nobody is ever around to appreciate it.

Hylda Baker (1909–82) was a British comedienne who established herself in northern music-hall tradition and in such films as *Saturday Night and Sunday Morning, Up the Junction* and *Nearest and Dearest*.

J.M. Barrie

The God to whom little boys say their prayers has a face very like their mother's.

J.M. Barrie (Sir James Matthew Barrie, 1860–1937) was a Scottish novelist and dramatist. He became editorial writer for the *Nottingham Journal* in 1883 but turning to fiction he had great success, particularly with *Peter Pan*, *Mary Rose* and *Dear Brutus*.

John Barrymore

The way to fight a woman is with your hat. Grab it and run.

John Barrymore (1882–1924) was a celebrated American stage and screen actor, brother of Ethel and Lionel Barrymore. He was an idol with a great 'profile' and became famous as a romantic movie star of the twenties, but later he squandered his talents in inferior comedies and developed an alcohol problem.

Brendan Behan

We have flower battles just as they do in Nice. Only here we throw the pots as well.
On the Dublin Festival, 10 July 1960

Brendan Behan (1923–64), Irish author and playwright, was a housepainter by trade. He started writing in 1951, achieving success in 1956 with his play *The Quare Fellow* which was based on his own prison experiences. Other works followed, including *Borstal Boy*, *The Hostage* and *Brendan Behan's Island*.

Hilaire Belloc

How did the party go in Portland Square?
I cannot tell you: Juliet was not there.
And how did Lady Gaster's party go?
Juliet was next to me, and I do not know.
Blinding Love

Hilaire Belloc (1870–1953) was the son of a French barrister and an English mother and became a natural-ized British citizen in 1902. He founded *The Eye Witness* in collaboration with Cecil Chesterton, with whom he wrote a political work entitled *The Party System*. His literary versatility is shown by his nonsense verse, historical studies, and satires.

Irving Berlin

We depend largely on tricks, we writers of songs. There is no such thing as a new melody.

Irving Berlin (1888–   ), an American composer of popular songs, wrote such hits as *Alexander's Ragtime Band*, *Always* and *Annie Get your Gun*. Born in Russia and named Israel Baline, he settled in America in 1893 and used Irving Berlin as a pseudonym.

Josh Billings

It is the little bits of things that fret and worry us; we can dodge an elephant, but we can't dodge a fly.

Consider the postage stamp; its usefulness consists in the ability to stick to one thing till it gets there.

There is one kind of laugh that I always recommend; it looks out of the eye first with a merry twinkle, then it creeps down on to its hands and knees and plays around the mouth like a pretty moth around the haze of a candle.

There are two things in this life for which we are never fully prepared: twins.

Josh Billings (1818–85) was the pseudonym of Henry Wheeler Shaw, an American humorous writer. His popular work *Josh Billings, His Sayings* depended for its humour on mis-spellings, puns, and malapropisms.

James Boswell

I never shall forget the indulgence with which he (Samuel Johnson) treated Hodge, his cat, for whom he himself used to go out and buy oysters, lest the servant having that trouble should take a dislike to the poor creature.

The Life of Samuel Johnson, Hodge the Cat

While the Dictionary was going forward, Johnson lived part of the time in Holborn, part in Gough Square, Fleet Street, and he had an upper room fitted up like a counting-house for the purpose in which he gave to the copyists their several tasks.

The words, partly taken from other dictionaries, and partly supplied by himself, having been first written down with spaces left between them, he delivered in writing their etymologies, definitions, and various significations.

The authorities were copied from the books themselves, in which he had marked the passages with a black-lead pencil, the traces of which could easily be effected.

I have seen several of them, in which that trouble had not been taken, so that they were just as when used by the copyists.

The Life of Samuel Johnson

James Boswell (1740–95) was a Scottish biographer and man of letters. He studied law but centred his ambition on literature and politics. He is most famous for his biography, *The Life of Samuel Johnson*. Their first meeting was in 1763, and this was followed in 1764 with the formation of the Literary Club, the original members of which included Reynolds, Burke and Goldsmith. Garrick and C.J. Fox joined soon after, and it was here that Boswell became so closely associated with Johnson and took great interest in the formation of his *Dictionary* (published in 1755).

Bessie Braddock

Right now the basic insecurity the workers feel is this; they are haunted by the spectre of the van driving up to the door to take away the TV set.

19.6.1955

Bessie (Elizabeth Margaret) Braddock JP (1899–1970) was Labour MP for the Exchange Division of Liverpool from 1945 onwards. She was the daughter of Mary Bamber JP and Hugh Bamber, and married John Braddock in 1922. For a time she was President of Liverpool Trades and Labour Council.

George Burns

It takes very little to turn me on. And sometimes when I think I'm turned on, I find out I'm not even plugged in.
Samuel Walton reporting in Saturday Evening Post

George Burns (1898–) first made his name in vaudeville as a dancer. Then he teamed up with Gracie Allen, and together they toured the USA and Europe, making their radio debut with the BBC. In 1976 he received an Academy Award for Best Supporting Actor in the film *The Sunshine Boys*.

Hoagy Carmichael

The trouble with doing nothing is that you can never take any time off.

Hoagy Carmichael (1899–1982) was an American song composer and lyricist, best known for his *Stardust* and *In the Cool, Cool, Cool of the Evening*. He was also a slow-speaking actor of light supporting roles, usually involving his singing at the piano. He wrote two autobiographies, *The Stardust Road* and *Sometimes I Wonder*.

Enrico Caruso

The requisite of a singer — a big chest, a big mouth, ninety per cent memory, ten per cent intelligence, lots of hard work, and something in the heart.

Enrico Caruso (1873–1921) was an Italian operatic tenor. Born in Naples, he made his first appearance on the stage there at twenty-one, and later achieved great success in Milan in Puccini's *La Bohème*. Subsequently he won world-wide fame and appeared in many European and American cities.

G.K. Chesterton

The home is not the one tame place in the world of adventure. It is the one wild place in the world of rules and set tasks.

There are no rules of architecture for a castle in the clouds.

A yawn is a silent shout.

Old Noah he had an ostrich farm, and fowls on the largest scale...
He ate his egg with a ladle in an egg-cup big as a pail.
And the soup he took was Elephant Soup, and the fish he took was whale.
But they all were small to the cellar he took when he set out to sail.

Wine and Water

Gilbert Keith Chesterton (1874–1936) was a British author, born in London. He studied art, but quickly turned to journalism. In poetry his best work was in satire, particularly in his *Wine, Water and Song* and *The Ballad of the White Horse*. His most famous novels are those dealing with the adventures of the naive priest-detective, Father Brown.

Sir Winston Churchill

I have always been surprised to see some of our Bishops and clergy making such heavy weather about reconciling the Bible story with modern scientific and historical knowledge. Why do they want to reconcile them?

If you are the recipient of a message which cheers your heart and fortifies your soul, which promises you reunion with those you have loved in a world of larger opportunity and wider sympathies, why should you worry about the shape or colour of the travel-stained envelope; whether it is duly stamped, whether the date on the postmark is right or wrong?

These matters may be puzzling, but they are certainly not important. What is important is the message and the benefits to you of receiving it.

My Early Life

Sir Winston Leonard Spencer Churchill (1874–1965) was a descendant of the Duke of Marlborough. Churchill was born at Blenheim Palace, the elder son of Lord Randolph

11

Churchill and his American wife, Jenny Jerome. After a brilliant career and varying fortunes he became the great leader of the British people during the Second World War. His accomplishments included painting and literature, for which he won the Nobel Prize in 1953.

Confucius

If husband sent too often to doghouse, he go at last to cathouse.

Confucius (c550–478BC) is a Latinised form of K'ung Fu-tzu (K'ung the master) and this Chinese sage was born in Lu, a small state in what later became the province of Shangtun. His early years were spent in poverty, but at fifteen his mind was set on learning. Gradually he attracted a number of disciples to his system of cosmology, politics and ethics. He revised the ancient Chinese scriptures, and on his death was buried with great pomp.

Bette Davis

Morality to me is honesty, integrity, character. Old-fashioned words. There are new words now that excuse everything.

Give me the days of heroes and villains. The people you can bravo or hiss. There was a truth to them that all the slick credulity of today cannot touch.

How wonderful it would be to know again where we stand and which side we're on.

The Lonely Life

Bette Davis (1908–), the American actress and film star, was born Ruth Elizabeth Davis in Massachusetts. She entered films in 1930 and established her reputation with *Of Human Bondage*. Later films included *Dangerous* and *Jezebel*, both of which earned her Academy Awards. Her career has been an outstanding one and she has written two autobiographies, *The Lonely Life* (1962) and *Mother Goddam* (1975).

Marlene Dietrich

The average man is more interested in a woman who is interested in him than he is in a woman — any woman — with beautiful legs.

Marlene Dietrich (1901–   ) was born in Berlin as Maria Magdalena von Losch. A German singer-actress living in America for many years, she became a legend of glamour in films, being known particularly for her part in *The Blue Angel*.

Benjamin Disraeli

No, it is better not. She would only ask me to take a message to Albert.

> *Reply when it was suggested to him as*
> *he lay dying that he might like a visit*
> *from Queen Victoria*

Benjamin Disraeli (1804–81), first Earl of Beaconsfield, was the eldest son of Isaac D'Israeli, and received his literary training chiefly in his father's library. In 1837 he entered Parliament as member for Maidstone, and became leader of a small group called The Young England Party whose ideas are described in his novels *Coningsby* and *Tancredi*. In his final year as Prime Minister, he published his novel *Endymion*.

Dorothy Dix

Drying a widow's tears is one of the most dangerous occupations known to man.

Dorothy Dix (Dorothy Knight Waddy, 1909–70) was the second daughter of William Knight Dix. Educated at St Christopher's School, Hampstead, Lausanne University and University College London, she became a QC in 1957 and a County Court Judge in 1968. She acted as Deputy-Recorder of Deal in 1946, during the absence of Mr Christmas Humphries at the Tokyo War trials.

Thomas Edison

As a cure for worrying, work is better than whisky.

Thomas Alva Edison (1847–1931) was an American inventor. Born in Ohio of Dutch–Scottish parentage, he became first a newsboy and then a telegraph operator. His first invention was an automatic repeater for telegraphic messages, and this was followed by over one thousand others, including many devices for the distribution of light and power.

Albert Einstein

If A is success in life, the A equals X plus Y plus Z. Work is X; Y is play; and Z is keeping your mouth shut.

I also am a revolutionary, though only a scientific one.

Professor Albert Einstein (1879–1955) was a German–Swiss physicist, framer of the theories of relativity. After teaching at the Polytechnic School in Zurich he became a Swiss citizen and was appointed an inspector of patents at Berne. In his spare time he obtained his PhD at Zurich, and some of his papers on physics were of such a high standard that in 1909 he was given a chair of theoretical physics at the University. His first theory — the so-called special theory of relativity — was published in 1905, but in 1915 he issued his general theory. He received the Nobel Prize for physics in 1921 for his work in quantum theory.

George Eliot

You love the roses — so do I. I wish
The sky would rain down roses, as they rain
From off the shaken bush...
... Why will it not?
Then all the valley would be pink and white
And soft to tread on.

The Book of a Thousand Poems, Roses

George Eliot (1819–80) was the pseudonym of the British writer Mary Ann Evans. Born at Chilvers Coton, Warwickshire, she received a strictly evangelical upbringing but later moved to Coventry and was converted to free thinking. She became famous for her novels *Adam Bede*, *The Mill on the Floss* and *Silas Marner*, which were all set in her native county. Other novels followed; *Middlemarch* is regarded as her finest work and one of the greatest novels of the century.

Dame Edith Evans

As a young actress I always had a rule. If I didn't understand anything, I always said it as if it were improper.

Quoted by Robin May in 'The Wit of the Theatre'

Dame Edith Evans (1888–1976), the British actress, was well known for her versatility on the stage, but is famous for her portrayal of Lady Bracknell in *The Importance of Being Earnest*. She appeared in Shakespeare, Restoration comedy, Wilde and Shaw, as well as in films.

David Everett

Don't view me with a critic's eye,
But pass my imperfections by.
Large streams from little fountains flow,
Tall oaks from little acorns grow.

Lines written for a School Declamation

David Everett (1770–1813) was an American author. Born in Princetown, Massachusetts, he became a lawyer and journalist, and was the author of *Common Sense in Dishabille, Daranzel* (a play performed in 1798 and 1800) and several other works.

St Francis of Assissi

Lord, make us instruments of thy peace. Where there is hatred, let us sow love; where there is injury, pardon; where there is discord, union; where there is doubt, faith; where there is despair, hope; where there is darkness, light; where there is sadness, joy.

St Francis of Assissi (1162–1226) was the son of a wealthy Italian merchant. In his early twenties he gave away all his wealth and took up a life of poverty and service, which attracted many followers. Many stories are told of his ability to charm wild animals and to influence men in all walks of life.

Robert Frost

Home is the place where, when you have to go there, they have to take you in.

A poem begins in delight and ends in wisdom.

All men are born free and equal — free at least in their right to be different. Some people want to homogenize society everywhere. I'm against the homogenizers in art, in politics, in every walk of life. I want the cream to rise.
The Letters of Robert Frost to Louis Untermeyer.

Robert Lee Frost (1874–1963) was an American poet. Born in San Francisco, he farmed unsuccessfully in New Hampshire, but combined it with teaching and writing poetry. He sailed to England and established his reputation as the author of several books, then returned to America and won Pulitzer poetry prizes for *New Hampshire*, *Collected Poems*, *A Further Range* and *A Witness Tree*.

Zsa Zsa Gabor

Never despise what it says in the women's magazines; it may not be subtle, but neither are men.

Zsa Zsa Gabor (1919–   ) was born Sari Gabor. This glamorous international lady was Miss Hungary of 1936. She has since appeared in films of many nations, including *Lovely to Look At* (USA), *Lily* (USA), *Moulin Rouge* (GB), *Public Enemy Number One* (France) and *Diary of a Scoundrel* (USA).

Paul Getty

My formula for success? Rise early, work late, strike oil. If all the money and property in the world were divided up equally at say, three o'clock in the afternoon, by 3.30

there would already be notable differences in the financial conditions of the recipients. Within that first thirty minutes, some adults would have lost their share, some would have gambled theirs away, and some would have been swindled or cheated out of their portion, thereby making some others richer...

... The disparity would increase with growing momentum as time went on. After ninety days the difference would be staggering. And I'm willing to wager that, within a year or two at the most, the distribution of wealth would conform to patterns almost identical with those that had previously prevailed.

From his autobiography 'As I See It'

John Paul Getty (1892–1976) was an American oil millionaire. He was President of the Getty Oil Co from 1947 and founder of the J. Paul Getty Museum, California, which is noted for its eighteenth-century French furniture and tapestries, and an art collection ranging through the fifteenth to seventeenth centuries.

Johann Wolfgang von Goethe

It is not doing the thing we like to do, but liking the thing we have to do, that makes life blessed.

Give me the benefit of your convictions if you have any; but keep your doubts to yourself, for I have enough of my own.

Johann Wolfgang von Goethe (1749–1832) was a German poet, man of letters, statesman and philosopher. Born in Frankfurt-am-Main, he first discovered his poetic vocation while studying law at Leipzig and became famous, amongst other works, for his drama *Faust*.

Samuel Goldwyn

The reason so many people showed up at Louis B. Mayer's funeral was because they wanted to make sure he was dead.

Going to call him William? What kind of a name is that? Every Tom, Dick and Harry's called William. Why don't you call him Bill?

Yes, my wife's hands are very beautiful. I'm going to have a bust made of them.

If you can't give me your word of honour, will you give me your promise?

Samuel Goldwyn (1882–1974) was born of Jewish parents in Warsaw. As a Pole with an unpronounceable name, he arrived in the United States, and an immigration official named him 'Goldfish'. Eventually he realised the trick that had been played on him and changed it to Goldwyn. He founded the Goldwyn Pictures Corporation which later became the Metro-Goldwyn-Mayer Company in 1925. He is particularly famed for his witty 'Goldwynisms'.

Sir Edward Grey

The lamps are going out all over Europe; we shall not see them lit again in our lifetime.

Sir Edward Grey (First Viscount of Fallodon, 1862–1933) was the eldest son of Captain George Henry Grey. He was educated at Winchester and Balliol College, Oxford, and from 1895 was Under-Secretary for Foreign Affairs. From 1885 to 1916 he was MP for Berwick-on-Tweed, and was created Viscount of Fallodon in 1916.

François Guizot

Do not be afraid of enthusiasm. You need it. You can do nothing effectually without it.

François Pierre Guillaume Guizot (1787–1874) was a French statesman and historian. Born at Nîmes, he was a Protestant and from 1812 to 1830 was professor of history at the Sorbonne. He wrote about the history of civilisation and became Prime Minister in 1847.

Joseph Hall

Moderation is the silken string running through the pearl chain of all virtues.

Christian Moderation, Introduction

Joseph Hall (1574–1656) was Bishop of Exeter and Norwich. Educated at Ashby-de-la-Zouch and Emmanuel College, Cambridge, he published some satires which were attacked by Marston in 1601. He became chaplain to Henry, Prince of Wales, and chaplain to Lord Doncaster in France; also he accompanied James I to Scotland. Impeached and imprisoned in 1642, he had his episcopal revenues sequestered in 1643 and was expelled from his palace in 1647.

Oscar Hammerstein II

A sudden beam of moonlight, or a thrush you have just heard, or a girl you have just kissed, or a beautiful view through your study window is seldom the source of an urge to put words on paper. Such pleasant experiences are likely to obstruct and delay a writer's work.

Oscar Hammerstein II (1895–1960) was an immensely successful lyricist who wrote many stage musicals, usually with Richard Rodgers. Together they achieved fame with such shows as *The King and I*, *South Pacific* and *The Sound of Music*, and are well-remembered for such songs as *Oh What a Beautiful Morning* and *Younger than Springtime*.

Minnie Louise Haskins

And I said to the man who stood at the gate of the year: 'Give me a light that I may tread safely into the unknown'. And he replied: 'Go out into the darkness and put your hand into the hand of God. That shall be to you better than light and safer than a known way.'

From 'God Knows', quoted by King George VI in his Christmas broadcast on 25 December 1939

Minnie Louise Haskins (1875–1957) was educated at Clarendon College, Clifton, the London School of Economics and the University of London. For some years she did educational work in India, and in the First World

War she was Supervisor of Women's Employment and Industrial Welfare work. She published a number of works, including *The Desert, Through Beds of Stone* and *The Gate of the Year*.

William Hazlitt

The rule for travelling abroad is to take our common sense with us, and leave our prejudices behind.

Table Talk

William Hazlitt (1778–1830) dabbled in portrait painting, but took to writing on the advice of Coleridge. He then went to London where he contributed numerous articles to various periodicals on art, drama and literary criticism. He became famous for, amongst other works, *Table Talk* and *The Spirit of the Age*.

Paul Hindemith

People who make music together cannot be enemies, at least not while the music lasts.

A Composer's World

Paul Hindemith (1895–1963) was a German composer. A fine viola player, he led the Frankfurt Opera Orchestra at twenty, and taught composition at the Berlin Hochschule for Music from 1927 to 1933, when the modernity of his *Philharmonic Concerto* led to a Nazi ban. In 1939 he went to America where he taught at Yale and in 1952 he became professor of musical theory at Zurich.

Alfred Hitchcock

Suspense is a matter of knowledge. If a bomb unexpectedly goes off in a film — that's surprise. But if the audience knows a bomb will go off in five minutes, and the hero on screen doesn't know it — that's suspense.

Alfred Hitchcock (1899–1981) was a British film director and a master of suspense. His notable films include *The Thirty-nine Steps, Rebecca, Rope, Strangers on a Train, Rear Window, Vertigo, Psycho* and *The Birds*.

Oliver Wendell Holmes

Nine times out of ten, the first thing a man's companion knows of his short-comings is from his apology.

If I had a formula for bypassing trouble, I would not pass it round. Trouble creates a capacity to handle it. I don't embrace trouble; that's as bad as treating it as an enemy. But I do say meet it as a friend, for you'll see a lot of it and had better be on speaking terms with it.

Oliver Wendell Holmes (1809–94) was an American writer. Born in Cambridge, Massachusetts, he became professor of anatomy at Dartmouth and later at Harvard. Later still with Lowell he founded the *Atlantic Monthly* and published *The Professor at the Breakfast Table*.

Thomas Hood

Never go to France
Unless you know the lingo.
If you do, like me,
You will repent, by jingo.

Family Word Finder

Thomas Hood (1799–1845) was a British poet. Born in London, he entered journalism and edited periodicals which included *Hood's Magazine*. Best known for his comic verse, he also wrote serious poems such as *Song of the Shirt* and *Bridge of Sighs*.

Sir Fred Hoyle

Outer space isn't remote at all. It's only an hour's drive away if your car could go straight upward.

Sir Fred Hoyle (1915–   ), the British astronomer, was educated at Cambridge and became Plumian professor of astronomy and experimental philosophy there in 1958. He became famous for his radio talks and science fiction as well as his contribution to cosmological theory (continuous creation) and such books as *Nuclei* and *Quasars*.

Victor Hugo

Common-sense is in spite of, not the result of, education.

Victor Marie Hugo (1802–85) was a French poet, novelist, and dramatist. Born at Besançon, the son of one of Napoleon's generals, he established himself as the leader of French Romanticism with the verse play *Hernani*. Later plays included *Lucrece Borgia*. In 1851 he was banished for opposing Louis Napoloen's coup d'état and settled in Guernsey, but on the fall of the Empire in 1870 he returned to France and became a senator.

T.H. Huxley

The rung of a ladder was never meant to rest upon, but only to hold a man's foot long enough to enable him to put the other somewhat higher.

Thomas Henry Huxley (1825–95) was a British scientist, humanist, and agnostic thinker. Born at Ealing, he graduated in medicine and for several years was surgeon to *HMS Rattlesnake* on a surveying expedition in the South Seas. Following the publication of *The Origin of Species* in 1859, he won fame as 'Darwin's bulldog', and for many years was the most prominent and popular champion of evolution.

Samuel Johnson

Kindness is generally reciprocal; we are desirous of pleasing others because we receive pleasure from them.

Adversity is the state in which a man most easily becomes acquainted with himself, being especially free from admirers then.

My master whipt me very well. Without that, Sir, I should have done nothing! While Hunter was flogging the boys unmercifully, he used to say — 'And this I do to save you from the gallows.'

There is no private house in which people can enjoy themselves as well as in a capital tavern. Let there be ever so much elegance, ever so much desire that everybody should be easy; in the nature of things it cannot be; there must be some degree of care and anxiety...

The master of the house is anxious to entertain his guests; the guests are anxious to be agreeable to him; and no man, but a very impudent dog indeed, can so freely command what is in another man's house, as if it were his own...

Whereas, at a tavern, there is a general freedom from anxiety. You are sure you are welcome; and the more noise you make, the more trouble you give, the more good things you call for, the welcomer you are...

No servants will attend you with the alacrity which waiters do, who are excited by the prospect of an immediate reward in proportion as they please...

On Inns

Samuel Johnson (1709–84) was an English lexicographer, author and critic. Born in Lichfield, he was educated at Lichfield Grammar School and Pembroke College, Oxford. He entered the service of Edward Cave the printer and in 1747 issued the 'plan' of his *Dictionary* for Lord Chesterfield's consideration but it was not published until 1755. Johnson was one of the founders of the Literary Club in Fleet Street, and it was there that he became so closely associated with Boswell, his biographer.

Yousuf Karsh

Great men are often lonely. But perhaps that loneliness is part of their ability to create. Character, like a photograph, develops in darkness.

Yousuf Karsh (1908–), the Canadian photographer, was born in Armenia. He made use of strong highlights and shadows, and in 1933 opened his own studio in Ottawa. His 'bulldog' portrait of Churchill in the Second World War brought him world fame.

Helen Keller

Security does not exist in nature, nor do the children of men as a whole experience it. Avoiding danger is no safer in the long run than exposure. Life is either a daring adventure or nothing.

On Security

With my three trusty guides, touch, smell and taste, I make many excursions into the borderland of experience... Nature accommodates itself to every man's necessity. If the eye is maimed, so that it does not see the beauteous face of the day, the touch becomes more poignant and discriminating. Nature proceeds through practice to strengthen and augment the remaining senses.

Life with Three Senses, The World I Live In

When we do the best that we can, we never know what miracle is wrought in our life or in the life of another.

Helen Adams Keller (1880–1968) was an American author who became famous because of her great triumph over adversity. At only nineteen months old she suffered an illness through which she lost the senses of sight and hearing, and consequently became dumb. After a painful period of frustration she was helped by the skill and patience of Anne Sullivan Macy, who taught her how to speak. Under Anne's expert guidance Helen Keller graduated with honours at Radcliffe College in 1904, and later published several books. Her first meeting with her teacher was described in William Gibson's play *The Miracle Worker* (1959) which was made into a film in 1962.

Lord Kilmuir

When the ruins of Pompeii were uncovered, dice were found. It is a sad commentary on the unvarying conditions of human nature that some of the dice were loaded.

Sayings of the Week

Lord Kilmuir (David Patrick Maxwell Fife, 1900–67), British lawyer and Conservative politician, was called to the Bar in 1922. He became an MP in 1935, Solicitor-General from 1942–5 and Attorney General in 1945 during the Churchill governments. At the Nuremberg trials he was deputy to Sir Hartley Shawcross and for most of the time conducted the British prosecution. He was Home Secretary from 1951 to 1954 and Lord Chancellor from 1954 to 1962. In 1954 he was created Viscount and in 1962 Earl.

Martin Luther King

I have a dream that one day on the red hills of Georgia, the sons of former slaves and the sons of former slave-owners will be able to sit down together at the table of brotherhood.
Speech at Civil Rights March on Washington, 28 August 1963

I have a dream that my four little children will one day live in a nation where they will not be judged by the colour of their skin, but by the content of their character.
Speech at Civil Rights March on Washington, 28 August 1963

Injustice anywhere is a threat to justice everywhere.
Letter from Birmingham Alabama Jail, published in the Atlantic Monthly, August 1963

I just want to do God's will. And he's allowed me to go to the mountain. And I've looked over, and I've seen the promised land... So I'm happy tonight. I'm not worried about anything. I'm not fearing any man.
Speech at Birmingham Alabama on 3 April 1968, the evening before his assassination

Martin Luther King (1929–68) was an eloquent black Baptist minister who, from the middle 1950s until his assassination in April 1968, led the first mass civil rights movement in United States history. He achieved world-wide recognition when he was awarded the 1964 Nobel Prize for Peace for his application of the principle of non-violent resistance — patterned after India's Mahatma Gandhi — in the struggle for racial equality in America.

Stephen Leacock

Many a man in love with a dimple makes the mistake of marrying the whole girl.

Writing is not hard. Just get paper and pencil, sit down and write it as it occurs to you. The writing is easy — it's the occurring that's hard.

Stephen Leacock (1869–1944), a British humorous writer born in Hampshire, lived in Canada from 1876 and became head of the department of economics at McGill University, Montreal, from 1908 until 1936. He published works on politics and economics, and studies of Mark Twain and Dickens, but is best known for his humorous writings. These include *Literary Lapses*, *Nonsense Novels* and *Frenzied Fiction*.

C.S. Lewis

Friendship is born at the moment when one person says to another, "What! You too? I thought I was the only one."

Reality is usually something you could not have guessed. That is one of the reasons I believe Christianity. It is a religion you could not have guessed. If it offered us just the kind of universe we had always expected, I should feel we were making it up. It has just that queer twist about it that real things have.

Clive Staples Lewis (1898–1963) was a British scholar. From 1954 to 1963 he was professor of Medieval and Renaissance English at Cambridge, and his books include the remarkable medieval study *The Allegory of Love* and the science fiction *Out of the Silent Planet*. He also wrote some essays in popular theology, the autobiographical *Surprise by Joy*, and a number of books for children.

Abraham Lincoln

I don't know who my grandfather was. I am much more concerned to know what his grandson will be.

Abraham Lincoln (1809–65) was the sixteenth President of the USA. Born in a Kentucky log cabin, he was almost entirely self-educated but qualified as a lawyer. Entering politics, he sat first as a Whig, then joined the new Republican Party in 1856, and became President on a minority vote in 1860. Between his election and his inauguration seven slave states seceded from the Union, and these were followed by four more. Civil War soon raged and Lincoln became extremely unpopular. In 1863 his proclamation freed slaves in the Confederate territory. Five days after Robert E. Lee's surrender Lincoln was assassinated by a Confederate fanatic.

David Lloyd George

Don't be afraid to take a big step if one is indicated. You can't cross a chasm in two small jumps.

David Lloyd George (1863–1945) was a Welsh Liberal statesman. Born in Manchester, the son of a teacher, he became an MP, making his reputation as a fiery Radical and Welsh Nationalist. The First World War brought him fame as the dominating figure in the Cabinet — he was Prime Minister of the Coalition Government in 1916 — and after the war he was among those primarily responsible for the Versailles peace settlement.

André Maurois

The difficult part of an argument is not to defend one's opinion but rather to know it.

André Maurois (1885–1967) was the pseudonym of the French author Emile Herzog. In the First World War he was attached to the British Army, and his essays *Les Silences du Colonel Bramble* (1918) give humorously sympathetic observations on the British character.

Yehudi Menuhin

The price of freedom for all musicians, both composers and interpreters, is tremendous control, discipline and patience: but perhaps not only for musicians. Do we not all find freedom to improvise, in all art, in all life, along the guiding lines of discipline?

Theme and Variations

Above other arts, music can be possessed without knowledge. Being an expression largely of the subconscious, it

27

has its direct routes from whatever is in our guts, minds and spirits, without need of a detour through the class-room.

Unfinished Journey

Yehudi Menuhin (1916–) is an American violinist. Born of Russian–Jewish parentage, he gave his first concert at the age of eight. Two years later he made a tour of Europe, dazzling the critics by his maturity and freshness of approach. Retiring for a period of intensive study, he then achieved such a depth of interpretation, particularly in the Elgar and Beethoven concertos, that he soon became known as one of the world's greatest players. In 1963 he founded the Yehudi Menuhin School at Stoke D'Abernon, Surrey, a boarding school for talented musicians, which is the only one of its kind outside Russia.

George Meredith

I expect that Woman will be the last thing civilized by man.

The Ordeal of Richard Feverel

I've studied men from my topsy-turvy
Close, and, I reckon, rather true.
Some are fine fellows: some, right scurvy:
Most a dash between the two.

Juggling Jerry

She is steadfast as a star,
And yet the maddest maiden:
She can wage a gallant war,
And give the peace of Eden.

Marian

Lovely are the curves of the white owl sweeping,
Wavy in the dusk lit by one large star.

Love in the Valley

George Meredith (1828–1909) was a British novelist and poet. Born in Portsmouth, he was educated in Germany and then articled to a London solicitor but he soon entered journalism. He published *Poems* and *The Shaving of Shagpat* but his first realistic psychological novel, *The Ordeal of Richard Feverel*, was followed by a number of others including *The Egoist, Diana of the Crossways* and *The Amazing Marriage*. Later he wrote *Modern Love* and *Poems and Lyrics*.

Alice Meynell

Thou art like silence unperplexed,
A secret and a mystery
Between one footfall and the next.

To The Beloved

Flocks of the memories of the day draw near
The dovecot doors of sleep.

At Night

Alice Christiana Gertrude Meynell (1847–1922) was a British poet and essayist whose essays include *Rhythm of Life* and *Second Person Singular*. Her youngest son, Sir Francis Meynell, founded the Nonsuch Press and was knighted in 1946.

George Mikes

You can keep a dog; but it is the cat who keeps people, because cats find humans useful domestic animals. A dog will flatter you but you have to flatter a cat. A dog is an employee; the cat is a freelance.

How to be Decadent

George Mikes (1912–   ) was born in Budapest and has been President of PEN in exile for many years. He has also been theatrical critic on Budapest newspapers and London correspondent of Budapest newspapers for some time. He has published a number of humorous books including *How to be an Alien, How to Scrape Skies, Wisdom for Others, Milk and Honey, Down with Everybody* and *Shakespeare and Myself*.

John Milton

The cock with lively din
Scatters the rear of darkness thin,
And to the stack, or the barn-door,
Stoutly struts his dames before...

Right against the eastern gate
Where the great sun begins his state...

Meadows trim with daisies pied,
Shallow brooks and rivers wide;
Towers and battlements it sees
Bosom'd high in tufted trees...

Towered cities please us then,
And the busy hum of men...

And pomp, and feast, and revelry,
With mask, and antique pageantry,
Such sights as youthful poets dream
On summer eves by haunted stream...

L'Allegro

John Milton (1604–74) was born in Bread Street, Cheapside, the son of a scrivener and composer of music. Educated at St Paul's School and Christ's College, Cambridge, he became a BA in 1629 and an MA in 1632. After leaving Cambridge he lived with his father at Horton in Buckinghamshire, and whilst there he read the classics and prepared himself for his vocation as a poet. After the execution of Charles I, he published *Tenure of Kings and Magistrates* and was then appointed Latin secretary to the newly-formed Council of State. He became blind but retained his post as Latin secretary until the Restoration when he was arrested and fined. He was soon released but lost the greater part of his fortune.

James Monroe

A little flattery will support a man through great fatigue.

James Monroe (1758–1831) was fifth President of the USA. Born in Virginia he served in the War of Independence, was Minister to France from 1794 to 1796, and during 1803 negotiated the Lousiana Purchase. He was Secretary of State from 1811–15, was elected President in 1816 and again in 1820. His name is associated with the Monroe Doctrine expressed in his message to Congress in 1823.

Montaigne

When I play with my cat, who knows if I am more of a pastime to her than she is to me?

There is no torture that a woman would not endure to enhance her beauty.

Michel Eyquem de Montaigne (1533–92), the French essayist, was born at the Château de Montaigne near Bordeaux. He studied law and became a councillor of Bordeaux. For a time he frequented the Court of Francis II but eventually retired to his estates and wrote several volumes of *Essays* revealing his insatiable intellectual curiosity. He became preoccupied with the subject of death after the premature death of his friend La Boétie.

Montesquieu

Civility costs nothing and buys everything.

Charles Louis de Secondat Montesquieu (1689–1755) was a French philosophical historian. Born near Bordeaux, he became adviser to the Bordeaux government in 1714 but, after the success of his *Lettres persanes* in 1721, he adopted a literary career.

Ogden Nash

One man's remorse is another's reminiscence.

I kind of like the playful porpoise,
A healthy mind in a healthy corpus.
He and his cousin, the playful dolphin,
Why, they like swimmin' like I like golphin.

The panther is like a leopard,
Except it hasn't been peppered.
Should you behold a panther crouch,
Prepare to say Ouch.
Better yet, if called by a panther,
Don't anther.

The truth I do not stretch or shove
When I state the dog is full of love.
I've also proved, by actual test
A wet dog is the lovingest.

Everyone But Thee and Me, The Dog

If you should happen after dark
To find yourself in Central Park,
Ignore the paths that beckon you
And hurry, hurry to the zoo.
And creep into the tiger's lair.
Frankly, you'll be safer there.

Everyone But Thee and Me, City Greenery

Ogden Nash (1902–71) was born in Rye, New York.
This American poet published numerous volumes of
humorous verse of impeccable technique and quietly
puncturing satire.

Beverley Nichols

Why this passion for shaking people out of ruts? I am
devoted to ruts. Moreover, most of the people who are in
ruts are much nicer, and much happier, than the people
who are not. Ruts are the wise old wrinkles that civiliza-
tion has traced on the earth's ancient face.

The Gift of a Home

Beverley Nichols (1901–   ) is a British writer, educated
at Marlborough College and Balliol College, Oxford. For
a time he was President of the Oxford Union and Editor of
Isis and he was also founder and editor of the Oxford
Outlook. Amongst other works he published his autobiography, *Twenty-Five*, in 1926.

Denis Norden

Middle age is when, wherever you go on holiday, you
pack a sweater.

Denis Norden (1922–   ) is a British writer and comedian, educated at Craven Park School. He served in the RAF from 1942–45 and afterwards became staff writer in a variety agency. He first teamed up with Frank Muir in 1947, and is a very experienced and successful radio and television broadcaster.

Kathleen Norris

From birth to eighteen a girl needs good parents. From eighteen to thirty-five she needs good looks. From thirty-five to fifty-five a woman needs personality; and from fifty-five on the old lady needs cash.

Kathleen Norris (1880–1966) was born in San Francisco, California, and spent her early years in Mill Valley, a small mountain-village in California. She was the daughter of James Alden Thompson and Josephine Moroney and married Charles Gilman Norris who died in 1945. Kathleen became librarian, social worker and writer, producing many novels. Her last one was *Family Gathering*, published in 1959.

Ovid

Take rest; a field that has rested gives a beautiful crop.

Ovid (43BC–AD17) was a Roman poet, whose full name was Publius Ovidius Naso. He was born at Sulmo and studied rhetoric in Rome in preparation for a legal career but soon turned to literature. In AD8 he was banished by Augustus to Tomi on the Black Sea, where he died. This punishment was supposedly for his immoral *Ars Amatoria* but was probably due to some connection with Julia, the profligate daughter of Augustus.

Ignacz Jean Paderewski

Piano playing is more difficult than statesmanship. It is harder to awake emotions in ivory keys than it is in human beings.

Ignacz Jean Paderewski (1860–1941) was a Polish pianist, composer and statesman. The son of a Polish patriot, he gained European and American fame after his debut in Vienna in 1887 and became a noted exponent of Chopin. During the First World War he raised money in America for the relief of Polish war victims and organised the Polish army in France. In 1919 as Prime Minister he represented the newly independent Poland at the Peace Conference.

Thomas Paine

The sublime and the ridiculous are often so nearly related, that it is difficult to class them separately. One step above the sublime makes the ridiculous, and one step above the ridiculous makes the sublime again.

The Age of Reason

Thomas Paine (1737–1809) was born in Thetford, but he went to America and there published *Common Sense* which was an influential republican pamphlet. He fought for the colonists in the War of Independence. In 1787 he returned to England and soon published *The Rights of Man*, which was an answer to Burke's *Reflections on the Revolution in France*, but in 1792 he was indicted for treason. He escaped to France, where he represented Calais in the Convention but, after narrowly escaping the guillotine, he regained his seat after the fall of Robespierre. In 1793 he published *The Age of Reason*, and eventually returned to America, where he died.

Dorothy Parker

Guns aren't lawful,
Nooses give:
Gas smells awful:
You might as well live.

Résumé

Down from Caesar past Joynson-Hicks
Echoes the warning, ever new;
Though they're trained to amusing tricks,
Gentler, they, than the pigeon's coo,
Careful, son, of the cursed two —
Either one is a dangerous pet;
Natural history proves it true —
Women and elephants never forget.

Ballade of Unfortunate Mammals

That woman speaks eighteen languages, and she can't say 'no' in any of them.

Dorothy Parker (1893–1967) was an American writer, born in the West End of New Jersey into the famous Rothschild family. She became Mrs Alan Campbell, and wrote verse and a number of short stories, quickly establishing a reputation for an acid wit and scathing comment.

Johann Heinrich Pestalozzi

To change people you must love them. Your influence reaches only as far as your love.

Johann Heinrich Pestalozzi (1746–1827) was born at Zurich and became a Swiss educationalist. He established an experimental school at Burgdorf in 1799, and moved it to Yverdon in 1805.

HRH Prince Philip

It is no good shutting your eyes and saying 'British is Best' three times a day after meals, and expecting it to be so.

29 April 1956

I have been wet and frozen, and fried in the sun. I have walked for miles through fields and over hills; I have frightened myself silly climbing to the top of rickety pigeon platforms, and I have sat shivering on the edge of a kale field in a blizzard.

To anyone with a conventional view of pleasure, to the town-living, comfort-loving commuter, the idea that there might be any thrill in wildfowling or rough shooting must seem too painfully ludicrous to be considered...

...Yet this is the stuff of natural history, this is a certain way to arouse enthusiasm for conservation. Without this introduction I would never have learnt about the sights and sounds of the country and the wilderness.

Published in Saturday Evening Post

HRH Prince Philip, Duke of Edinburgh (1921–   ) is a grandson of George I of Greece and a great-grandson of Queen Victoria. He was born in Corfu but raised in England and educated at Gordonstoun and Dartmouth Naval College. A naturalised British subject taking the surname of Mountbatten in March 1947, he married Princess Elizabeth (later Queen Elizabeth II) in Westminster Abbey, having the previous day received the title Duke of Edinburgh. In 1956 he founded the Duke of Edinburgh's Award Scheme to encourage creative achievement among young people.

Pablo Picasso

I do not seek — I find.

Pablo Ruiz Picasso (1881–1973) was a famous Spanish artist, son of art teacher José Ruiz Blasco and an Andalusian mother Maria Picasso Lopez, but he discontinued the use of the name Ruiz in 1898. Born at Malaga, he was a mature artist at ten, and at sixteen was holding his first exhibition. From 1901–4 he had his Blue Period, when he painted mystic distorted figures in blue tones, and followed this with his Rose Period, Cubism, etc. He was unique in the fertile vigour of his invention, and his exhibitions attracted a large popular following.

Plutarch

I don't need a friend who changes when I change and who nods when I nod; my shadow does that much better.

Plutarch (AD46–120) was born in Greece at Chacronea, lectured on philosophy at Rome and was appointed procurator of Greece by Hadrian. His *Parallel Lives* consists of pairs of biographies of Greek and Roman soldiers and statesmen, followed by comparisons between the two. North's translation inspired Shakespeare's Roman plays.

Edgar Allan Poe

Helen, thy beauty is to me
Like those Nicaean barks of yore,
That gently, o'er a perfumed sea,
The weary, wayworn, wanderer bore
To his own native shore.

On desperate seas long wont to roam
Thy hyacinth hair, thy classic face,
Thy Naiad airs, have brought me home
To the glory that was Greece
And the grandeur that was Rome.

To Helen

Edgar Allan Poe (1809–49) was an American author born in Boston but orphaned at the age of two. He was brought up by a Mr and Mrs Allan, whose surname he used as a middle name from 1824. After a period of poverty and alcoholism and the death of his wife, he concentrated on writing poems of melancholy beauty. His reputation rests on short stories of horrific atmosphere such as *The Fall of the House of Usher*, and certain detective stories such as *The Gold Bug* and *The Murders in the Rue Morgue* which laid the foundations of modern detective fiction.

Alexander Pope

Where'er you find 'the cooling western breeze',
In the next line, it 'whispers through the trees'.
If crystal streams 'with pleasing murmurs' creep,
The reader's threaten'd (not in vain) with 'sleep'.

Essay on Criticism

True ease in writing comes from art, not chance,
As those move easiest who have learn'd to dance.

Essay on Criticism

Come, lovely nymph, and bless the silent hours,
When swains from shearing seek their nightly bowers;
When weary reapers quit the sultry field,
And, crowned with corn, their thanks to Ceres yield,
This harmless grove no lurking viper hides,
But in my breast the serpent Love abides.

Sylvan Delights

'Yet Chloe sure was formed without a spot'
Nature in her then erred not, but forgot.
'With every pleasing, every prudent part,
Say, what can Chloe want? — She wants a heart.'

Characters, Chloe

Virtue may choose the high or low degree,
'Tis just alike to Virtue, and to me;
Dwell in a monk, or light upon a king,
She's still the same, beloved, contented thing.

The Triumph of Vice

Alexander Pope (1688–1744) was the son of a Roman Catholic linen-draper of London. His health was ruined and his figure distorted by a severe illness at the age of twelve but he showed his literary skill in his *Pastorals* which were written when he was sixteen. He became friendly with William Wycherley, the English dramatist, who introduced him to London. Pope's *Essay on Criticism* (1711) made him known to Joseph Addison's circle and his *Messiah* was published in *The Spectator* in 1712. *Rape of the Lock* appeared in Lintot's *Miscellanies* in the same year and was republished in an enlarged form in 1714. Pope wrote *Ode for Music on St Cecilia's Day* in 1713 but it was not very successful. He moved away from Joseph Addison's circle and became a member of the 'Scriblerus Club', an association which included Swift, Gay, Arbuthnot, Atterbury and others. In 1715 he issued the first volume of his translation in heroic couplets of Homer's *Iliad*.

Dilys Powell

Society splits into cat-lovers and dog-lovers. For years I cared chiefly for cats. Later I came round to dogs as well — to dogs, I mean, as sharers of bed and board. A cat is a house guest. A dog joins the family. He makes friends for you, or at any rate, acquaintances. People one might never have spoken to greet one warmly; they know your dog's name when you remain anonymous.

Animals in My Life
Sunday Times, June 27 1976

Dilys Powell CBE (1901–) was *Sunday Times* film critic from 1939–76 and now reviews films for *Punch*. She is the author of several books, including *The Villa Ariadne*.

Enoch Powell

As I look ahead I am filled with foreboding. Like the Roman, I seem to see 'The River Tiber' foaming with much blood.

Speech at Birmingham, April 1968,
a reference to Virgil's 'Aeneid'

All political lives, unless they are cut off in mid-stream at a happy juncture, end in failure, because that is the nature of politics and of human affairs.

John Enoch Powell (1912–) was educated at King Edward's School, Birmingham, and Trinity College, Cambridge. He became Craven Travelling Student of 1933, Fellow of Trinity College, Cambridge, from 1934–38, and Professor of Greek in the University of Sydney, Australia, from 1937–9. He has been MP for South Down since 1974. Often an outspoken and controversial figure, Enoch Powell has held various appointments on the British General Staff, has been Parliamentary Secretary of the Ministry of Housing and Local Government, Financial Secretary to the Treasury, and Minister of Health.

J.B. Priestley

As a rule I like local accents, and have kept one myself. They make for a variety in speech and they give men's talk a flavour of the particular countryside to which at heart they belong. Standard English is like standard anything else — poor tasteless stuff.

English Journey

To travel swiftly in a closed car, as so many of us do nowadays, is to cut oneself off from the reality of the regions one passes through, perhaps from any sane reality at all. Whole leagues of countryside are only a roar and a muddle outside the windows, and villages are only like brick-coloured bubbles that we burst as we pass. Their life is temporarily as remote as the moon.

English Journey

Fountains enchant me — in the daytime, when the sunlight turns their scattered drops into diamonds; after dark when coloured lights are played on them, and the night rains emeralds, rubies, sapphires.

Essays

John Boynton Priestley (1894–   ), the prolific British novelist, was born in Bradford, the son of a schoolmaster. He was educated at Trinity Hall, Cambridge, and served in the First World War. He established his reputation as a novelist with *The Good Companions* and later wrote *Angel Pavement, Dangerous Corner, An Inspector Calls*, and other well-known plays.

Matthew Prior

Dear Chloe, how blubbered is that pretty face!
Thy cheek all on fire, and thy hair all uncurled.
Prithee, quit this caprice; and (as old Falstaff says)
Let us e'en talk a little like folks of this world.

How cans't thou presume thou hast leave to destroy
The beauties which Venus but lent to thy keeping?
Those looks were designed to inspire love and joy:
More ordinary eyes may serve people for weeping...

What I speak, my fair Chloe, and what I write, shows
The difference there is betwixt Nature and Art:
I court others in verse, but I love thee in prose;
And they have my whimsies, but thou hast my heart.

Answer to Chloe Jealous

Matthew Prior (1664–1721) was born in Dorset, the son of a joiner, and educated at Westminster School (under the patronage of Lord Dorset) and St John's College, Cambridge. He entered the diplomatic service in 1691, was appointed secretary to the ambassador at the Hague and employed in the negotiations for the Treaty of Ryswick. In 1697 this treaty ended the war between Great Britain, Austria, Spain and their allies on one side and France on the other. He joined the Tories and in 1711 was sent to Paris as a secret agent at the time of peace negotiations. The War of the Spanish Succession culminated in the Treaty of Utrecht (1713), popularly known as 'Matt's Peace'. On Queen Anne's death in 1714 he was imprisoned for two years. After his release a folio edition of his poems was brought out by his admirers, by which he gained the sum of four thousand guineas.

Francis Quarles

Even like two little bank-dividing brooks,
That wash the pebbles with their wanton streams,
And having ranged and searched a thousand nooks,
Meet both at length in silver-breasted Thames
Where in a greater current they conjoin:
So I my Best-Beloved's am, so he is mine.

Even so we met; and after long pursuit
Even so we joined; we both became entire;
No need for either to renew a suit,
For I was flax and he was flames of fire:
Our firm united souls did more than twine,
So I my Best-Beloved's am, so he is mine.

He gives me wealth, I give him all my vows;
I give him songs, he gives me length of days;
With wreaths of grace he crowns my conquering brows;
And I his temples with a crown of praise...
My Beloved is Mine and I am His

My soul, sit thou a patient looker-on;
Judge not the play before the play is done:
Her plot has many changes; every day
Speaks a new scene; the last act crowns the play.
Epigram

Francis Quarles (1592–1644) was a metaphysical poet. He went abroad in the suite of Princess Elizabeth, daughter of James I, on her marriage with the Elector Palatine, and wrote pamphlets in defence of Charles I, which led to the sequestration of his property. He is chiefly remembered for his *Emblems*, a book of short devotional poems which was published in 1635.

François Rabelais

A child is not a vase to be filled, but a fire to be lit.

François Rabelais (1494–1553) was a French author, born at Chinon, Touraine. He became a monk and, having studied medicine, lectured on anatomy. He wrote

41

several great works, particularly some satirical allegories which were laced with coarseness, broad humour and philosophy.

Sir Joshua Reynolds

It is allowed on all hands, that facts, and events, however they may bind the historian, have no dominion over the poet or the painter. With us, history is made to bend and conform to this grand idea of art...

These arts, in their highest province, are not addressed to the gross senses; but to the desires of the mind, to that spark of divinity which we have within.

Discourses, The Aims of Art

Sir Joshua Reynolds (1723–92), the British artist, was born near Plymouth. He went to London at the age of seventeen and was apprenticed to Thomas Hudson, a mediocre portrait painter. For several years he was active as a portrait painter in London and Plymouth, but in 1749 he went abroad to complete his studies. After living in Rome and other Italian cities he settled in London and became the most famous portrait painter of his day and the first President of the Royal Academy.

Sir Ralph Richardson

We actors are the jockeys of literature. The dramatist writes the plays; we try to make them run.

Sir Ralph David Richardson (1902–) was born in Cheltenham and has had an extensive career on stage since 1921 and in films from 1933. He also achieved great success as actor–director of the Old Vic from 1944 to 1947.

La Rochefoucauld

Before strongly desiring anything, we should look carefully into the happiness of its present owner.

François, Duc de la Rochefoucauld (1613–80) was born in Paris, became a soldier and took part in the wars of the Fronde. His later years were divided between the Court

and literary society. He is best known for his work
Réflexions, Sentences et Maximes Morales (1665).

Will Rogers

It's great to be great, but it's greater to be human.

Will Rogers (1879–1935) was an American rustic comedian. For a time he was in the Ziegfeld Follies, but later
became famous for many films, including *Almost a
Husband, The Gay Caballero* and *The Strongest Man in the
World*.

Christina Rossetti

Raise me a dais of silk and down;
Hang it with vair and purple dyes;
Carve it in doves and pomegranates,
And peacocks with a hundred eyes...

Work it in gold and silver grapes,
In leaves and silver fleurs-de-lys;
Because the birthday of my life
Is come, my love is come to me.

A Birthday

Does the road wind up hill all the way?
Yes, to the very end.
Will the day's journey take the whole long day?
From morn to night, my friend.
But is there for the night a resting-place?
A roof for when the slow, dark hours begin...

Uphill

Christina Georgina Rossetti (1830–94), the British poet
and sister of the poet and artist Dante Gabriel Rossetti,
was a devout Anglican. She produced much popular lyric
and religious verse.

Gioachino Antonio Rossini

Give me a laundry list and I'll set it to music.

Gioachino Antonio Rossini (1792–1868) was an Italian
composer. Born at Pesaro, his first success was the opera

Tancredi, but three years later his *Il Barbiere di Siviglia* was produced at Rome. At first it was a failure. Rossini had a fertile composition period from 1815–23 during which time he produced twenty operas. After *Guillaume Tell* (1829) he gave up writing opera and spent his time in Bologna and Paris.

Jean-Jacques Rousseau

He who is slowest in making a promise is most faithful in its performance.

Jean-Jacques Rousseau (1712–78) was a French philosopher who was born in Geneva. He was apprenticed to a lawyer and engraver but ran away and for some time led the wandering life described in his *Confessions*. Later he published *A Discourse on The Origin of Inequality* which made him famous.

Bertrand Russell

Every man who has acquired some unusual skill enjoys exercising it until it has become a matter of course, or until he can no longer improve himself. This motive to activity begins in early childhood: a boy who can stand on his head becomes reluctant to stand on his feet.

A great deal of work gives the same pleasure that is to be derived from games of skill.

The work of a lawyer or a politician must contain in a more delectable form a great deal of the same pleasure that is to be derived from playing bridge. Here, of course, there is not only the exercise of skill but the outwitting of a skilled opponent.

A man who can do stunts in an aeroplane finds the pleasure so great that for the sake of it he is willing to risk his life.

The Exercise of Skill from
'The Conquest of Happiness'

Bertrand Arthur William Russell (1872–1970) was a British philosopher and mathematician. Born at Trelleck, the grandson of the first Earl Russell (Lord John Russell), he was educated at Trinity College, Cambridge, where he specialised in mathematics and became a lecturer. His pacifist attitude in the First World War lost him the lectureship, and he served six months in prison for an article he wrote in a pacifist journal. After the war he went to Russia, China and the USA, where he taught at many universities. Later he returned to England and wrote many books, being awarded the OM in 1949 and the Nobel Prize for literature in 1950. On the death of his brother in 1931 he succeeded to the earldom, becoming the third earl.

George Santayana

We live experimentally, moodily, in the dark; each generation breaks its eggshell with the same haste and assurance as the last, pecks at the same indigestible pebbles, dreams the same dreams, or others just as absurd, and if it hears anything of what former men have learnt by experience, it corrects their maxims by its first impressions.

England is pre-eminently a land of atmosphere. A luminous haze permeates everywhere, softening distances, magnifying perspective, transfiguring familiar objects, harmonizing the accidental, making beautiful things magical and ugly things picturesque.

Mists prolong the most sentimental and soothing of hours, the twilight, through the long summer evenings and the whole winter's day.

Soliloquies in England

George Santayana (1863–1952) was a Spanish philosopher. Born in Madrid, he graduated at Harvard where he taught the history of philosophy from 1889 to 1911. He wrote a number of books on philosophy, several volumes of poems and the novel *The Last Puritan*.

Robert Schumann

In order to compose, all you need is to remember a tune that nobody else has thought of.

Robert Schumann (1810–56) was a German musician. Born at Zwickau, Saxony, he taught at Leipzig Conservatoire and was musical director at Düsseldorf from 1850 to 1853. As a composer he excelled in pianoforte compositions and in *Lieder*. His piano concerto Opus 54 and sonatas Opus 11 and 22 are particularly famous.

Albert Schweitzer

Many women were dying in childbirth. The elders warned them never to see a doctor, that it would bring bad luck. How can I gain power over these old witches? I thought.

Then I hit on the idea of presenting each baby born at my hospital with a little bonnet and dress. By sheer bribery, my power was established, and pregnant women have flocked to the hospital ever since.

Reader's Digest, September 1980

Albert Schweitzer (1875–1965), the French theologian, was also an organist and missionary surgeon. He founded a hospital in 1913 at Lambarene, Republic of Gabon. He remained there apart from the brief intervals spent giving recitals of organ music, mainly Bach, in order to raise funds for his medical work. He was awarded the Nobel Peace Prize in 1952.

William Shakespeare

Heat not a furnace for your foe so hot
That it do singe yourself.

King Henry VIII

To gild refined gold, to paint the lily,
To throw a perfume on the violet,
To smooth the ice, or add another hue
Unto the rainbow...
Is wasteful and ridiculous excess.

King John

What's in a name? That which we call a rose
By any other name would smell as sweet.

Romeo and Juliet

Take honour from me, and my life is done.

King Richard II

The man that hath no music in himself
Nor is not moved with concord of sweet sounds,
Is fit for treasons, stratagems and spoils —
The Merchant of Venice

How far that little candle throws his beams!
So shines a good deed in a naughty world.
The Merchant of Venice

It is a wise father that knows his own child.
The Merchant of Venice

The devil can cite Scripture for his purpose.
The Merchant of Venice

If all the year were playing holidays,
To sport would be as tedious as to work.
King Henry IV Part I

Out of this nettle, danger, we pluck this flower, safety.
King Henry IV Part I

Be not afraid of greatness: some are born great, some
achieve greatness, and some have greatness thrust upon
them.
Twelfth Night

Everyone can master a grief but he that has it.
Much Ado About Nothing

Cowards die many times before their deaths;
The valiant never taste of death but once.
Julius Caesar

William Shakespeare (1564–1616) was born at Stratford-upon-Avon and educated at the Free Grammar School. He left Stratford in about 1582 and went to London where he joined a company of players and soon became established as an actor and playwright. His plays brought him immediate fame. His output was prolific and his collected works as published today contain 37 plays, 2 long poems, and 154 sonnets. The plays are divided into 17 comedies, 10 histories, and 10 tragedies. He basked in the favour of Queen Elizabeth I and her successor, King James I, but eventually ceased to write and retired once again to Stratford-upon-Avon.

George Bernard Shaw

People are always blaming their circumstances for what they are. I do not believe in circumstances. The people who get on in this world are the people who get up and look for the circumstances they want, and if they cannot find them, make them.

Success covers a multitude of blunders.

If you cannot get rid of the family skeleton, you may as well make it dance.

George Bernard Shaw (1856–1950), the son of a civil servant, left Ireland and came to London, where he became a brilliant debater among the Fabians. He wrote five novels and then became a successful playwright. His comedy *Pygmalion* was written especially for his great friend Mrs Patrick Campbell. Other plays include *Man and Superman, Heartbreak House* and *St Joan*. He won the Nobel Prize for literature in 1925.

Bishop Fulton Sheen

Each of us comes into life with fists closed, set for aggressiveness and acquisition. But when we abandon life our hands are open; there is nothing on earth we need, nothing the soul can take with it.

Bishop Fulton Sheen (1895–1979) was an American Roman Catholic prelate and auxiliary bishop of New York from 1951 to 1966. He achieved widespread influence by his radio *Catholic Hour* and television programmes.

Percy Bysshe Shelley

Like winged stars the fire-flies flash and glance,
Pale in the open moonshine, but each one
Under the dark trees seems a little sun,
A meteor tamed: a fixed star gone astray
From the silver regions of the Milky Way
                    To Maria Gisborne in England, from Italy

Music, when soft voices die,
Vibrate in the memory;
Odours, when sweet violets sicken,
Live within the sense they quicken...

Rose leaves, when the rose is dead,
Are heaped for the beloved's bed;
And so my thoughts, when thou art gone,
Love itself shall slumber on.

Percy Bysshe Shelley (1792–1822) was born at Field Place, Sussex, went to Eton and later to Oxford, but with his friend and fellow student James Hogg was expelled for being the author of a pamphlet entitled *The Necessity of Atheism*. His *Alastor* was published in 1816. In that same year he began his friendship with Byron, and about this time he wrote his *Hymn to Intellectual Beauty* and *Mont Blanc*. In 1818 Shelley left England for Italy, where he translated Plato's *Symposium* and finished *Rosalind and Helen*. In Rome in 1819, he was stirred to indignation by the political events in England, in particular the Peterloo affair, which persuaded him to write his *Mask of Anarchy*, an indictment of Castlereagh's administration. The Shelleys then moved to Pisa where he wrote some of his finest lyrics including *Ode to the West Wind, To a Skylark* and *The Cloud*. He was drowned while sailing near Spezia but just before his death he wrote more of his beautiful lyrics and a number of love poems inspired by Jane Williams.

Jean Christian Sibelius

Pay no attention to what the critics say. A statue has never been erected in honour of a critic.

Jean Christian Sibelius (1865–1957) was a Finnish composer. His father wanted him to take up the law, but instead he studied the violin and composition at Helsingfors and went on to Berlin and Vienna. In Britain and the USA he was recognised as a major composer and became known for his orchestral *En Saga* and *Karelia*, the tone poems *Finlandia* and *Night Ride and Sunrise*, the appealing *Valse Triste*, and seven symphonies.

Philip Dormer Stanhope

Never seem more learned than the people you are with. Wear your learning like a pocket-watch and keep it hidden. Do not pull it out to count the hours, but give the time when you are asked.

Letters to his Son

Philip Dormer Stanhope (1694–1773), fourth Earl of Chesterfield, was an opponent of Walpole and upon the latter's death became Lord Lieutenant of Ireland in 1745 and a Secretary of State in 1746. He was associated with Swift, Pope, and Bolingbroke and is remembered chiefly for his letters to his son.

Robert Louis Stevenson

So long as we love we serve; so long as we are loved by others, I would almost say we are indispensable.

Keep your fears to yourself but share your courage.

Robert Louis Stevenson (1850–94) entered Edinburgh University in 1867 and studied engineering, but he soon abandoned it for the law. An illness of the lungs led to his frequent journeys in search of health, and his *Inland Voyage* described a canoe tour in Belgium and France. His *Travels with a Donkey* followed the following year. Although very ill he contributed to many periodicals and wrote a number of essays, short stories, and fragments of travel and autobiography. He became famous because of his *Treasure Island, The Strange Case of Dr Jekyll and Mr Hyde, Kidnapped, Catriona, The Black Arrow* and *The Master of Ballantrae*. He also wrote some remarkable poetry, which was collected in *A Child's Garden of Verses* and *Underwoods*.

Leopold Stokowski

It is not necessary to understand music;
It is only necessary that one enjoy it.

Leopold Stokowski (1887–1977) was an American conductor. Born in London of British and Polish parentage, he studied at the Royal College of Music and was conductor of the Cincinnati Symphony Orchestra be-

50

tween 1909 and 1912, and of the Philadelphia Orchestra from 1913 to 1936, becoming an American citizen in 1915. An outstanding experimentalist, he introduced much contemporary music into the United States and appeared in a number of films, including Walt Disney's *Fantasia*.

Gladys Swarthout

A bright smile has compensated for many a vocal flaw in a concert.

Gladys Swarthout (1904–69) was an American opera singer. She also acted in a number of films, notably *Rose of the Rancho*, *Give us this Night*, *Champagne* and *Romance in the Dark*.

Jonathan Swift

The time is not remote when I
Must by the course of nature die:
When I foresee my special friends
Will try to find their private ends:
Though it is hardly understood
Which way my death can do them good...

...thus methinks I hear 'em speak:
'See, how the Dean begins to break,
Poor gentleman he droops apace,
You plainly find it in his face;
That old vertigo in his head
Will never leave him till he's dead...

Besides, his memory decays,
He recollects not what he says,
He cannot call his friends to mind,
Forgets the place where last he dined,
Plies you with stories o'er and o'er —
He's told them fifty times before
                    Verses on the Death of Doctor Swift by himself

Jonathan Swift (1667–1745) was born in Dublin and educated at Kilkenny Grammar School. A cousin of Dryden, he was admitted to the household of Sir William Temple in Moor Park near Farnham, where he acted as

Secretary. While there he wrote a number of Pindarics. Returning to Ireland he was ordained in 1694, but went back to Sir William and edited his correspondence. He also wrote *The Battle of the Books* and *A Tale of a Tub*.

Upon the death of Sir William, Swift went back to Ireland and was given a prebend in St Patrick's, Dublin. In 1713 he was made Dean of St Patrick's and from there he wrote the famous Drapier Letters. In 1726 he wrote *Gulliver's Travels*, which was really a satire on parties and statesmen, but soon it became a classic of children's literature. Nearly all Jonathan Swift's writings were published anonymously and it is possible that the £200 he received for *Gulliver's Travels* was the only payment he ever had.

Jack Tanner

The shop steward is a little like an egg.
If you keep him in hot water long enough, he gets hard-boiled.

Jack (Frederick John Shirley) Tanner (1889–1965) was born in Whitstable. He was President of the Amalgamated Engineering Union from 1939–54, and was awarded the CBE in 1954. In 1943 he became Member of the TUC General Council, and was President from 1953–54.

Alfred, Lord Tennyson

There is sweet music here that softer falls
Than petals from blown roses on the grass,
Or night-dews on still waters between walls
Of shadowy granite, in a gleaming pass.

Here are cool mosses deep
And thro' the moss the ivies creep,
And in the stream the long-leaved flowers weep,
And from the craggy ledge the poppy hangs in sleep.

The Lotus blooms below the barren peak:
The Lotus blows by every winding creek:
All day the wind breathes low with mellower tone:
Thro' every hollow cave and alley lone.

The Song of the Lotus-Eaters

Alfred, first Baron Tennyson (1809–92) was educated at Trinity College, Cambridge, where be became friendly with A.H. Hallam. He won the chancellor's medal for English verse in 1829 with a poem called *Timbuctoo*. In 1832 Tennyson travelled with Hallam on the Continent, but Hallam died in 1833. Tennyson immediately began *In Memoriam* expressing grief for his dead friend. This was followed by many poems and *The Idylls of the King*.

Harry S. Truman

Everybody has the right to express what he thinks. That, of course, lets the crackpots in. But if you cannot tell a crackpot when you see one, then you ought to be taken in.

Harry S. Truman (1884–1972) was an American states-man who was President between the years 1945–53. As Democratic Vice-President he took the office of President on the death of Franklin D. Roosevelt. He autho-rised the use of the first atomic bomb on Japan which devastated the city of Hiroshima, but was instrumental in ending the war against Japan. Truman implemented the Marshall Plan to aid the recovery of post-war Europe and the 'Truman Doctrine'.

Peter Ustinov

The sound of laughter has always seemed to me the most civilized music in the universe.

from 'Dear Me'

To be gentle, tolerant, wise and reasonable requires a goodly portion of toughness.

Peter Ustinov (1921–) is a British actor-dramatist. Born in London, he has ventured into almost every aspect of film and theatre life. He has written plays, being sometimes author, director, producer and princip-al actor in them. In 1963 he became joint director of the Nottingham Playhouse.

Sir John Vanbrugh

Good manners and soft words have brought many a difficult thing to pass.

Sir John Vanbrugh (1664–1726) was an English dramatist and architect. Born in London, he designed Blenheim Palace and the first Haymarket Theatre, London.

Ralph Vaughan-Williams

My advice to all who want to attend a lecture on music is don't. Go to a concert instead.

Ralph Vaughan-Williams (1872–1958) was a British composer who was born in Gloucester and studied at Cambridge and the Royal College of Music. He learnt much from Max Bruch in Berlin and Ravel in Paris. He wrote a number of symphonies, and in 1951 his operatic morality *The Pilgrim's Progress* was performed for the Festival of Britain. Later works included *Sinfonia Antartica* which was used in the film *Scott of the Antarctic*, and a ninth symphony. He received the OM in 1935.

Alfred de Vigny

Silence alone is great; all else is feebleness.
La Mort du Loup

Alfred de Vigny (1797–1863) was a French poet. Born at Loches, he joined the army at sixteen and had twelve years' service. His first volume of poems appeared in 1822 and was followed by his prose romance *Cinq Mars*. His drama *Chatterton* showed his interest in England where he lived for some years, after marrying an Englishwoman in 1828.

Publius Vergilius Maro Virgil

We cannot all do all things.
Eclogues

Happy he who has been able to learn the causes of things.
Georgics

But meanwhile...time is flying that cannot be recalled.
Georgics

Not ignorant of ill do I learn to aid the wretched.
Aeneid

I fear the Greeks even when they bring gifts.

Aeneid

From one piece of villainy judge them all.

Aeneid

A fickle and changeable thing is woman ever.

Aeneid

Virgil (Publius Vergilius Maro, 70–19BC), the Roman poet, was born near Mantua and eulogized his own yeoman class in his poems. He was patronized by Maecenas and his *Eclogues* (ten pastoral poems) appeared in 37BC. These were followed in 30BC by the *Georgics*, confirming him as the chief poet of the age. The last years of his life were spent in composing the *Aeneid*, an epic poem in twelve books intended to glorify the Julian dynasty, whose head was Augustus. An apparent forecast of the birth of Christ in the fourth *Eclogue* led to his acceptance as an 'honorary' Christian by the medieval Church and in popular legend he became a powerful magician.

Voltaire

If God did not exist, it would be necessary to invent him.
  Letters: To the Author of the Book of the Three Imposters

In this country (England) it is good to kill an admiral from time to time, to encourage the others.
  Candide, In allusion to the shooting of Admiral Byng

This agglomeration which was called and which still calls itself the Holy Roman Empire was neither holy, nor Roman, nor an Empire.

I disapprove of what you say, but I will defend to the death your right to say it.

Attributed

Voltaire (1694–1778) was the pseudonym of the French writer François-Marie Arouet. Born in Paris, the son of a notary, he adopted his pseudonym when he had already started writing poetry while still at his Jesuit seminary. His early essay offended the authorities and during the years 1716–26 he was twice imprisoned in the Bastille and thrice exiled from the capital for having written libellous political verse. Later in life he was at the Court of Frederick the Great who had long admired him, but the association ended in deep enmity and Voltaire established himself near Geneva. He is remembered for a number of works, but particularly for *Candide* and the tragedy *Irene*.

Lewis Wallace

Beauty is altogether in the eye of the beholder.

The Prince of India

Lewis Wallace (1827–1905) was a US general and novelist. He served in the Mexican and Civil Wars and subsequently became governor of New Mexico and minister to Turkey. He wrote the historical novels *The Fair God* and *Ben-Hur*.

Horace Walpole

Here lies Fred
Who was alive and is dead:
Had it been his father,
I had much rather.
Had it been his brother,
Still better than another:
Had it been his sister,
No-one would have missed her.

Had it been the whole generation,
Still better for the nation;
But since 'tis only Fred,
Who was alive and is dead
There's no more to be said.

*Written after the death of Frederick,
Prince of Wales in 1751*

Strawberry Hill is a little plaything house that I got out of Mrs Chenevix's shop, and is the prettiest bauble you ever saw. It is set in enamelled meadows, with filigree hedges.

Letters: To Conway, 8 June 1747

Horace Walpole (1717–97) was the fourth son of Sir Robert Walpole. He travelled in France and Italy with Thomas Gray and later he settled at Strawberry Hill, Twickenham, where he established a printing press. Here he printed Gray's two Pindaric odes and his own *Anecdotes of Painting in England*. In 1764 he published his Gothic story *The Castle of Otranto*, but it is on his *Letters* that Walpole's literary reputation rests. They are said to be remarkable both for their charm and their autobiographical, social and political interest.

Izaak Walton

Look to your health; if you have it, praise God, and value it next to a good conscience; for health is the second blessing that we mortals are capable of; a blessing that money cannot buy.

Compleat Angler, Part 1 Ch 21

Izaak Walton (1593–1683) was an English author born in Stafford. He settled in London as an ironmonger and wrote short biographies of his friends Donne, Hooker, Sir Henry Wotton and George Herbert. He is well-known for his book *The Compleat Angler*, the location of which was the River Lea near London.

Isaac Watts

Let dogs delight to bark and bite,
For God hath made them so:
Let bears and lions growl and fight,
For 'tis their nature too.

But, children, you should never let
Such angry passions rise:
Your little hands were never made
To tear each other's eyes.

Divine Songs for Children,
Against Quarrelling

Isaac Watts (1674–1748) was the son of a Nonconformist schoolmaster and is remembered as the author of *Divine Songs for Children*. He also wrote a number of hymns, some of which have obtained a wide popularity. These include '*O God, our help in ages past*' and '*When I survey the wondrous cross.*'

Evelyn Waugh

The great charm in argument is really finding one's own opinion, not other people's.

Evelyn Arthur St John Waugh (1903–66) was a British novelist. Educated at Oxford, he later published studies of Edmund Campion and Ronald Knox. His novels achieved fame, particularly *The Loved One* and *Brideshead Revisited* which was recently televised.

Orson Wells

In Italy for thirty years under the Borgias they had warfare, terror, murder, bloodshed, but they produced Michelangelo, Leonardo da Vinci, and the Renaissance. In Switzerland, they had brotherly love, they had five hundred years of democracy and peace. And what did that produce? The cuckoo-clock.

> *(Orson Wells added these words to the Graham Greene–Carol Reed script of 'The Third Man')*

Orson Wells (1915–) is known as an ebullient actor–writer–producer–director with stage and radio experience. In 1938 he panicked the whole of America with a vivid radio version of *The War of the Worlds*, and in 1970 he was awarded an Academy Award for 'supreme artistry and versatility in the creation of motion pictures'.

Gilbert White

Many horses, though quiet with company, will not stay one minute in a field by themselves; the strongest fences cannot restrain them. My neighbour's horse will not only not stay by himself abroad, but he will not bear to be alone in a strange stable without discovering the utmost impatience, and endeavouring to break the rack and manger with his fore feet.

> *Sociable Animals, The Natural History of Selborne*

Gilbert White (1720–93), the English naturalist, was born at Selborne, Hampshire. He took orders in 1747 and in 1751 retired to his birthplace where he wrote

Natural History and Antiquities of Selborne which has become a classic. His home, 'The Wakes', was opened as a museum and library in 1955.

Ella Wheeler Wilcox

Laugh and the world laughs with you,
Weep, and you weep alone.
For the sad old earth must borrow its mirth
But has trouble enough of its own.

Solitude

Have you heard of the terrible family They,
And the dreadful venomous things They say?
Why, half of the gossip under the sun
If you trace it back you will find begun
In that wretched house of They.

Ella Wheeler Wilcox (1850–1919) was an American poet and journalist. She was described as 'the most popular poet of either sex and of any age read by thousands who never open Shakespeare'. She began to publish poems in 1872 and her last volume, *Poems of Affection*, was published posthumously.

John Wilmot, Earl of Rochester

Were I (who to my cost already am
One of those strange, prodigious creatures, man)
A spirit free to choose, for my own share,
What case of flesh and blood I pleased to wear,
I'd be a dog, a monkey or a bear,
Or anything but that vain animal
Who is so proud of being rational.

Homo Sapiens

John Wilmot, Earl of Rochester (1647–80), was a British poet who showed gallantry at sea in the Second Dutch War. He spent much of his time at Court where he established a reputation for debauchery. His poems include many graceful lyrics and some powerful satires, the best of which is said to be *A Satire Against Mankind*.

Acknowledgements and Sources

Boscombe (Bournemouth) Reference Library
Bournemouth Central Reference Library
New Milton (Hants) Reference Library
Winton (Bournemouth) Reference Library

Collins' Dictionary of People and Places
Concise Oxford Dictionary of Quotations
Everyman's Dictionary of Quotations and Proverbs
Family Word Finder
Gilbert Harding's Book of Happiness
Hutchinson's New Twentieth Century Encyclopaedia
International Who's Who
New Oxford Book of English Verse 1250–1950
Pear's Cyclopaedia
Quote — Unquote (Nigel Rees)
Reader's Digest Library
The Book of a Thousand Poems
Who's Who
Who Was Who

Index of Authors

Holmes, Oliver Wendell	(1809–94)	21
Hood, Thomas	(1799–1845)	21
Hoyle, Sir Fred	(1915–)	21
Hugo, Victor	(1802–85)	22
Huxley, T.H.	(1825–95)	22
Johnson, Samuel	(1709–84)	22
Karsh, Yousuf	(1908–)	23
Keller, Helen	(1880–1968)	24
Kilmuir, Lord	(1900–67)	24
King, Martin Luther	(1929–68)	25
Leacock, Stephen	(1869–1944)	25
Lewis, C.S.	(1898–1963)	26
Lincoln, Abraham	(1809–65)	26
Lloyd George, David	(1863–1945)	27
Maurois, André	(1885–1967)	27
Menuhin, Yehudi	(1916–)	27
Meredith, George	(1828–1909)	28
Meynell, Alice	(1847–1922)	29
Mikes, George	(1912–)	29
Milton, John	(1604–74)	30
Monroe, James	(1758–1831)	30
Montaigne, Michel Eyquem de	(1533–92)	31
Montesquieu	(1689–1755)	31
Nash, Ogden	(1902–71)	31
Nichols, Beverley	(1901–)	32
Norden, Denis	(1922–)	32
Norris, Kathleen	(1880–1966)	33
Ovid	(43BC–AD17)	33
Paderewski, Ignacz Jean	(1860–1941)	33
Paine, Thomas	(1737–1809)	34
Parker, Dorothy	(1893–1967)	34
Pestalozzi, Johann Heinrich	(1746–1827)	35
HRH Prince Philip	(1921–)	35
Picasso, Pablo	(1881–1973)	36
Plutarch	(AD46–120)	36
Poe, Edgar Allan	(1809–49)	37
Pope, Alexander	(1688–1744)	37
Powell, Dilys	(1901–)	38
Powell, Enoch	(1912–)	39
Priestley, J.B.	(1894–)	39
Prior, Matthew	(1664–1721)	40
Quarles, Francis	(1592–1644)	41
Rabelais, François	(1495–1553)	41
Reynolds, Sir Joshua	(1723–92)	42
Richardson, Sir Ralph	(1902–)	42
La Rochefoucauld	(1613–80)	42

Rogers, Will	(1879–1935)	43
Rossetti, Christina	(1830–94)	43
Rossini, Gioachino Antonio	(1792–1868)	43
Rousseau, Jean-Jacques	(1712–78)	44
Russell, Bertrand	(1872–1970)	44
Santayana, George	(1863–1952)	45
Schumann, Robert	(1810–56)	45
Schweitzer, Albert	(1875–1965)	46
Shakespeare, William	(1564–1616)	46
Shaw, George Bernard	(1856–1950)	48
Sheen, Bishop Fulton	(1895–1979)	48
Shelley, Percy Bysshe	(1792–1822)	48
Sibelius, Jean Christian	(1865–1957)	49
Stanhope, Philip Dormer	(1694–1773)	50
Stevenson, Robert Louis	(1850–94)	50
Stokowski, Leopold	(1887–1977)	50
Swarthout, Gladys	(1904–69)	51
Swift, Jonathan	(1667–1745)	51
Tanner, Jack	(1889–1965)	52
Tennyson, Alfred Lord	(1809–92)	52
Truman, Harry S.	(1884–1972)	53
Ustinov, Peter	(1921–)	53
Vanbrugh, Sir John	(1664–1726)	53
Vaughan-Williams, Ralph	(1872–1958)	54
de Vigny, Alfred	(1797–1863)	54
Virgil, Publius Vergilius Maro	(70–19BC)	54
Voltaire	(1694–1778)	55
Wallace, Lewis	(1827–1905)	56
Walpole, Horace	(1717–97)	56
Walton, Izaak	(1593–1683)	57
Watts, Isaac	(1674–1748)	57
Waugh, Evelyn	(1903–66)	58
Wells, Orson	(1915–)	58
White, Gilbert	(1720–93)	58
Wilcox, Ella Wheeler	(1850–1919)	59
Wilmot, John (Earl of Rochester)	(1647–80)	59